Encouraging Words

By
Melanie E. Thomas

ISBN-13: 978-0-615-98799-6
Printed in the United States of America
© Pending 2014 by Melanie E. Thomas

To My Family...for your love and support of me through all my ups and downs.

To Pastor Gary K. Patterson of Eagle's Nest Covenant Church…for giving me the first platform in which I could utilize my gift of poetry.

To Thomas Robinson...for your encouragement, your prayers, and support. Thank you for being obedient to the prompting of the Lord.

To the entire Price Family of Crenshaw Christian Center...for the example as well as the teaching of Faith which has strengthened me in my walk with God.

Table of Contents

Dedication.. 5
Worship
      Words of Worship........................... 7
      Anointed Worship........................... 8
      Consuming Fire............................... 9
      O God.. 10
      Thank You!..................................... 11
Relationship
      A Life Without Barriers.................... 13
      Unfaithful Heart............................. 14
      Lukewarm..................................... 15
      Master, Train Me............................ 16
      Use Me.. 17
      Tug of War..................................... 18
      A Love to Hold On To......................19
Fellowship
      It's Never Easy............................... 21
      When You Leave............................ 22
      A Prayer For My Family.................... 23
      The Most Expensive Gift................... 24
Testimony
      Joy Unspeakable............................ 27

This book is dedicated to my fellow brothers and sisters in Christ. I pray that these poems will encourage you in time of weakness, comfort you in time of sorrow, fill you with joy in knowing God's love for you, and admonish you to live a life that is pleasing to God.

Worship

Words of Worship

How can I thank you for Your great sacrifice
that freed me from the bonds of sin?
To know that while I may lose some battles,
the war I am bound to win.
You created me along with everything
in the heavens and on the earth.
All these things and those to come,
You predestined unto its birth.
Like a father, You guide and lead me
with unconditional love.
Wanting for me an abundant life
that can only come from You above.
As a child I came to you,
with eyes full of tears.
Like a parent, You healed my hurts
and calmed all of my fears.
When I got older, I strayed
from the path that I was given.
I looked for things to fill my life,
to find that life wasn't worth living.
I am seeking You now, not for your hand
but for your face instead.
Striving to put off the old man;
the old man is dead.
Your face, Your lap, Your arms,
all of You I seek to see.
Wisdom and knowledge of You I want,
as proof of Your spirit inside of me.
I desire to be Your servant,
shining Your light wherever You direct.
I am striving for transparency,
so the brightness I won't affect.
My God, my Lord, my Savior
and all that You are to me,
I praise You with a grateful heart
and love you with all that's in me.

Anointed Worship

Here I am, Lord.
Kneeling at your feet.
My hands I raise to you
For your attention I entreat.

My praise I pour out
From the depths of my soul.
To others, my mind is fragmented.
To You, my mind is whole.

For when I worship you wholeheartedly
Giving my best to you,
I in return receive the greatest gift of all –
That gift being You.

As my praise is poured out
And the cloud of gratefulness thickens the air
I am then covered by the dew of Your grace
And Your presence is felt everywhere.

So, the anointing of my praise
Though it is being poured out for You
Has fallen upon me in return
As Your love falls on me too.

Consuming Fire

I feel a fire in me
Whose flames grow higher
As it feeds on words of truth.
And the more heat I feel
It lessens life's appeal
As my control is pulled from the roots.

Prayer, praise and worship
Stoke the fire
And build up its warmth.
Sacrifice, solitude and service
Are like kindling that's
Thrown on the hearth.

Sometimes the world tries
To come in and douse out
The flames.
And it doesn't help
That my sinful flesh and Satan
Have the same aim.

My hope is that with
The Holy Spirit's help
My life will be rearranged.
And that the Lord will come in
To burn the chaff
And bring about a change.

So, Lord I pray
Come fan the flames
And consume me all the more.
Making me as pure as gold
And shiny to reflect
Your light from shore to shore.

O God

O God, the Lover of my soul.
I seek your embrace to make me whole.
You promised me that you would stay.
From you I don't want to turn away.

O God, my Father and Mother.
The perfect parent; there is no other.
You watch over and care for me from above.
Your undeserved sacrifice is proof of your agape love.

O God, my Confidant and Friend.
The only one to stick with me through thick and thin.
When I am down, you lift me up.
You encourage me on when I think I've had enough.

O God, all these things and more you are.
Your attention to me makes me feel like a star.
My serving you is how it should be.
But, the more I serve you, the more you bless me.

Thank You!

God, for every breath you give me… Thank You!
God, for every step I take on my own… Thank You!
God, for every sound that I hear… Thank You!
God, for everything that I can see… Thank You!
God, for every aroma I can smell… Thank You!
God, for every caress I feel… Thank You!
God, for every morsel of food I eat… Thank You!
God, for every stitch of clothing I wear… Thank You!
God, for every song I sing… Thank You!
God, for every hug I receive… Thank You!
God, for every family member that puts up with me… Thank You!
God, for every friend that you send me… Thank You!
God, for every person you send me to minister to… Thank You!
God, for the skills and talents I have… Thank You!
God, for the patience to deal with others… Thank You!
God, for the love you put in my heart for others… Thank You!
God, for the joy you give in the midst of storms… Thank You!
God, for the peace you give in the midst of wars… Thank You!
God, for the grace you extended to me… Thank You!
God, for Your mercy… Thank You!
God, for Your loving kindness… Thank You!
God, for Your plan for my life… Thank You!
God, for Your salvation… Thank You!

For all that I should be grateful for, I am most especially grateful for Your love.

"For God so loved the world, that He gave His only begotten Son, that whoever believes in Him shall not perish, but have eternal life."
John 3:16 (NASB)

Relationship

A Life Without Barriers

Before I was saved, I knew not the love and plan
That God had for my life and that of every man.
For sin's barriers kept me from experiencing it.
Bringing only knowledge to fear my imperfection, rejection,
and punishment.

As long as I kept this barrier up on my side
And refused to knock it down because of pride,
The demands of God's justice, holiness, and perfection
Required my punishment, rejection, and devaluation.

Once I accepted Jesus as God's only provision for my sin
And answered the invitation from my Lord and Savior to come in,
The barrier on my side started to crumble and fall,
While the barrier on God's side could not be found at all.

The barrier on God's side was removed by Christ's death.
While the barrier on my side still had bricks left.
These bricks were thoughts and attitudes from experiences before
Which took time to change while I was being healed and restored.

Now the barriers are all gone without a trace.
For I have come into the knowledge of God's grace,
His total acceptance and forgiveness of my sins,
The fully applied result of Christ's atonement.

Unfaithful Heart

How can you love me so,
When you know just what I am?
What do you see in me?
What, pray tell, is your plan?

I am an unfaithful harlot,
Who seeks pleasure outside the home.
I pay you lip service when I say I love you,
For my heart continues to roam.

All my needs you have met,
And yet I yearn for more.
I keep searching for treasures
When you have them all in store.

I've taken your love for granted.
Didn't spend quality time with you.
How long will you put up with me
Before setting me away from you?

                              I love you, for you are mine.
                      I've known what you are from the start.
                          You do not see yourself as I do,
                                  You only see a part.

                          Everything that you have done
                            And all that you go through
                                Are all necessary
                          To bring out the best in you.

                              Love can only be by choice,
                      So I give you the freedom to choose.
                      I pray you hearken unto my voice
                          Before all you have, you lose.

                          My love will always be there
                              For that will never change.
                            It is only through your choices
                          That the end will be arranged.

Lukewarm

Neither hot nor cold
What meal tastes good when it's lukewarm?
Do we not prefer it to be hot or cold?
Neither weak nor strong
Who wants to root for the team that only wins half its games?
Do we not prefer to root for the underdog or the clincher?
Neither here nor there
Who wants to be stuck in an airport?
Would you not prefer to stay at home or get to your destination?
Neither for or against
Who likes to hear "I don't know. What do you want to do?" when asking for someone's opinion?
Would you not prefer to have an opinion that can validate your own or change it for the better?
Neither love nor hate
Who wants to be ignored except for times of need?
Would you not prefer to be appreciated for your value or left alone completely?
Neither blind nor seeing
Who wants to be criticized for faults but never complimented on achievements?
Would you not prefer that all comments be kept to the speaker or that the faults and achievements get equal focus?
Neither deaf nor hearing
Who likes to be cut off when they are responding to a question?
Would you not prefer to be able to answer completely or not be asked the question at all?
Being lukewarm causes more contention than if you have a definite position. No one can question who you are when they are certain of where you stand.

"I know your deeds, that you are neither cold nor hot; I wish that you were cold or hot. So because you are lukewarm, and neither hot nor cold, I will spit you out of My mouth." Revelation 3:15-16(NASB).

Master, Train Me

Master, when you found me I was young
And tended to go roundabout myself.
I did not know your voice
Nor how to take your direction.
As you cared for me, fed me, and disciplined me,
I learned your voice and what you expected of me.
Now, I find myself seeking your attention
By climbing on your lap and calling to you.
I eagerly seek your command.
Waiting for you to give me direction.
Do you want me to stay or go?
Do I lie down or stand up?
Do I speak or just listen?
Or, is this our time to play chase?
You smile and laugh with joy when I chase after you.
While running, I look back to make sure you are chasing after me.
I don't mind the stays that bind me to you,
Because it means that we are walking together.
When I can't find you, I sometimes tear up my surroundings,
But, you do not send me away.
You just discipline me in love.
Then allow me to come to you again.
When the day is done and it is time to rest
I sleep better when I am lying at your feet.
Thank you, Master, for taking me in
And for giving me a home.

Use Me

Use me Lord, I pray.
Let it not be just words to say.
Let my Faith take flight.
Not of me, but of Your might.
Guide my feet in your way.
That I may walk with You every day.

Use me Lord, I pray.
Let it not be just words to say.
May I see others as you do.
To know why they're so special to you.
That I may greet them in love.
And so, shine Your light from above.

Use me Lord, I pray.
Let it not be just words to say.
Guard my tongue when I speak.
That no word spoken would make others weak.
Let my mouth speak Your word.
That Your will be done when it is heard.

Use me Lord, I pray.
Let it not be just words to say.
Let me not take Your grace for granted.
Let there be fruit from this tree planted.
May my confession not be made in vain.
By only taking hold of Your name.

Use me Lord, I pray.
Let it not be just words to say.
I want to be known by You as just.
So, living by faith is a must.
To You, faith alone brings no satisfaction.
I must also put my faith in action.

So again I say, "Use me, Lord."

Tug of War

To the left
Don't want to go
Hard to fight
The pleasures I know
Can't give up
Can't give in
Don't want to die
Death comes with sin

To the right
Where I want to be
Struggling to become
What God wants of me
Won't stop now
Won't stop trying
I want to live
It's the cost of Christ's dying

In the middle is my soul
The arms of it are sore
Tired of the back and forth
Wishing for the end of its war
Must not quit
Must push on
This war won't be over
Until I reach heaven

A Love to Hold On To

To my love, my heart's desire
The thought of you makes my spirit soar higher
Gone are the days of angst and fear
The days of security and love are here
I've never felt this way before
I've searched all over, but never more
Now I rest in arms of joy
No more acting of playing coy
Standing strong and sure through it all
Knowing you'll keep me to never fall
I trust in you and what you say
You've proven yourself every day
Thank you for showering me with your love
You are a blessing from above

Now to the one who holds my heart
Though I don't worry we'll ever part
Should you leave I want you to know
I thank you for being God's vessel
Helping me to draw near to Him
By praying for you and praising Him
I've come to understand my call
Trusting and giving God my all
Knowing with all knowing that He's here with me
Whether through you or just in me
On this one thing I will stand
I'll hold to God's love and won't let go of His hand

Fellowship

It's Never Easy

It's never easy to suffer loss
Nor deal with a loved one's pain.
Words are difficult to come across
To comfort those who remain.

It's never easy to let them go,
No matter how prepared you are.
You'll look to everything you know
Just to keep from falling apart.

I offer you these words of hope
And pray their comfort bring.
The Lord above can help you cope,
And to your heart give healing.

It's in God's plan the life we live
And the time in which we die.
It's about the love from our lives we give
To those in need that tell why.

For, as we go through life,
We touch those whom we come across.
And show them through our pain and strife,
The joy to come from The Cross.

See, this earth is temporary
And it is not our true home.
So, we are here to gather the quarry
That belongs to the heavens to come.

Our goal is to be reunited
With the God who first loved us.
Don't be sad for those who are quieted
For they have reached that goal before us.

So, look forward to the day
When again you'll see their face.
As it will glow with shiny rays
While they stand inside Heaven's gates.

When You Leave

A beautiful smile
A quiet face
A sparkling laugh
A warm embrace

These are the things that I will miss
When you leave this place.

A beautiful life
An answered prayer
A sparkling light to shine on you
A warm heart that cares

These I pray you will find
When you leave this place.

Remember me when you leave
And never forget that I am here.
For smiles and hugs last only for a while
But, years last the memories and tears.

A Prayer For My Family
In Loving Memory of John H Gayton

Father in Heaven, to You I pray,
Comfort my family and friends today.
Let them remember the days of my life.
How I handled the times of good and strife.

May they see all the blessings You gave to me.
And thank You for the blessings to them be.
May they see my mistakes that I have made,
And pray for forgiveness for theirs today.

May they see the love You had for me,
And choose to receive the love You're offering.
Help them to walk in Your will,
While there's breath in their bodies still.

For life is not promised to be long.
One day you're here, the next you're gone.
I pray to see them all again.
Looking forward to the Family Reunion in Heaven.

The Most Expensive Gift

As I celebrate Christmas with family and friends,
I think on all the love that I have received.
And how through the year until the end,
Of past sorrows and pains I've been relieved.

I can't escape the joy that came,
From spending the time with those I love.
Singing songs of Jesus' name
And the heavenly visits from above.

Presents unwrapped to be assembled
For children impatiently waiting.
Food lined up upon the table
Served on platters with gold plating.

This occasion is known for the giving
Of gifts the heart desires.
But, the most expensive gift for the living
Can lift your spirits higher.

It is the most expensive gift,
For it requires more from you
Than any other gift you give
Because of whom you give it to.

The gift of love is great indeed,
And everyone wants to have it.
But, the gift of forgiveness is hard to give or receive
Because most of us are lacking in it.

Jesus was born out of love for man
God sacrificed him for us.
The ultimate price was paid due to sin
Because of God's gift of forgiveness.

Take hold of this gift and receive it gladly
But, be as eager to give it too.
For without it your state is sadly
As unforgiveness steals peace from you.

Testimony

Joy Unspeakable

I've been cheated out of house and home.
A wife and mother left all alone.
Left with just two little children.
Thank God for the blessing I was given.

Lied and schemed against for greed.
Offering love to those with hearts for money.
Not down on love, just a little more wary.
Thank God for knowledge that my loneliness is temporary.

No job, no church, no kids.
I left for the Skids.
Not without hope and full of faith.
Thank God for favor and His grace.

Things look up and getting better.
Lose sight of God? Never!
Praising Him through the good and the bad.
That's joy unspeakable that I have.

I enjoy writing poetry that encourages people in their walk with God. Most of my poems have been written because I was inspired by a sermon or a testimony. They are a piece of me. A thought that came from a revelation. An expression of feelings experienced. A message put on my heart to share with others. As I go through my walk of faith, I am moved to use poetry as my way of sharing my testimony. I haven't reached the end of my journey yet, so there will be more to come.

This book is my legacy to my sons, James and Jerald McNeil. They are my blessings from heaven.

Melanie E. Thomas

www.ingramcontent.com/pod-product-compliance
Lightning Source LLC
Chambersburg PA
CBHW070051070426
42449CB00012BA/3226